ILearn Education Club

PEP SCIENCE

For Grade 6

Textbook and Workbook

Name: _____

School: _____

Grade: _____

First Edition

Acknowledgement

ILearn Education Club wishes to express thanks to the teachers, editors and all other individuals who contributed to the production of the PEP Science Textbook and Workbook for Grade 6.

If we have involuntarily breached any copyright laws, we encourage you to contact us as soon as possible.
Please send your feedback to info@eiclub.net

Ellure Intelligence Club Limited
Ellure's ILearn Education Club
Kingston
Jamaica, West Indies
Tel: 615-7135-6
Website: eiclub.net

PEP SCIENCE FOR GRADE 6
TEXTBOOK AND WORKBOOK

First Edition 2020

CONTENTS

CHAPTER 1: THE ENVIRONMENT

The Environment is the surroundings in which an organism lives or operates. It includes all living and non-living things in a particular geographical area. Living things, such as plants and animals, interact with the environment and adapt to the conditions.

NATURAL ENVIRONMENT

The natural environment includes all living things and naturally occurring non-living things. Living things include: plants and animals. Naturally occurring non-living things include: rocks, soil and water. Non-living things can also be manmade such as: houses and airplanes.

Figure 1.1 living and non-living things

TYPES OF NATURAL ENVIRONMENT

There are different types of natural environments. These include: forest, wetland, desert, grassland, tundra and marine. Each environment is characterized by a set of characteristics that are unique to that environment. These characteristics include: vegetation, animal life, soil and climate. The following table lists some characteristics of three types of environment.

Characteristics	Marine	Rainforest	Desert
Vegetation	Shrubs	Trees	Shrubs
Soil	Sandy	Loam	Sandy
Climate	Warm with wet and dry season	Warm and wet	Hot and dry

Table 1.1 Characteristics of natural environments

Soil Types

One of the most important characteristics of an environment is the soil type. This determines the type of vegetation as well as the animal life that is able to thrive in the environment. There are four main soil types:

1. **Sand** - This type of soil is made up of large particles that have quick water drainage. It is nutrient poor and not suitable for growing crops.
2. **Silt** - Silt soil contains medium sized particles that have good drainage but is still able to hold moisture.
3. **Clay** - Clay is made up of tiny particles that have poor drainage. It is rich in nutrients but it is unsuitable for farming due to slow drainage.
4. **Loam** - This is a mixture of clay, sand and silt soils. It is very rich in nutrients and holds moisture. It is ideal for growing crops.

Science Experiment: Soil

In this experiment we will compare the soil from three different environments.

Procedure:

1. *Obtain soil samples from the beach, forest and your garden.*
2. *Observe the samples for particle size and texture and record your findings.*
3. *Cork a plastic funnel with cotton ball and add a fixed mass of each soil (about 50g) sample in three separate funnels.*
4. *Place the funnel in a measuring cylinder.*
5. *Add equal volume of water to each funnel and record the volume.*
6. *Measure the time taken for the water to pass through and the volume of water that passed through each soil sample. Compare the volumes of water before and after.*

Soil Experiment Setup

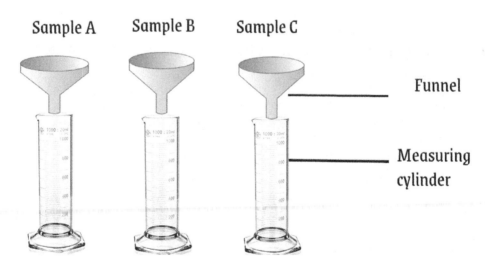

Figure 1.2 Soil experiment setup

Results

Complete the table with your results.

Variables	Beach soil	Garden soil	Forest soil
Initial volume			
Final volume			
Time taken			

Table 1.2 Results of the soil experiment

Use the results of the experiment to answer the following questions.

1. Which soil held the most water?

   _____

   _____

2. What do the results suggest about the water-holding capacity of each soil sample?

   _____

   _____

   _____

   _____

3. Predict which soil would be best for farming and explain your answer.

   _____

   _____

_____

_____

_____

4. Predict which soil is unsuitable for farming and explain your answer.

_____

_____

_____

_____

_____

MAN-MADE ENVIRONMENT

This comprise of all the buildings and infrastructures that are created by man.
These include:

Stadium

Image 1.1 Stadium

5

Town

Image 1.2 A town

House

Image 1.3 Interior of a house

Roads

Image 1.4 Highways with bridges

CONSERVING THE ENVIRONMENT

Environmental conservation is the practice of protecting the natural environment from adverse change or destruction.

Image 1.5 Environment conservation

Importance of the natural environment:

1. The environment provides a home for humans and other organisms.
2. It provides resources that are necessary for the survival of humans. These include food, clothing, water and medicine.
3. The environment helps to maintain a stable climate.

EFFECTS OF HUMAN ACTIVITIES ON THE ENVIRONMENT

Humans have a damaging effect on the environment. Due to over population, humans need more resources to survive. This forces them to engage in large scale farming, over fishing and huge construction projects. The results of these activities include:

1. Climate change
2. Pollution
3. Deforestation
4. Habitat destruction
5. Loss of biodiversity
6. Ozone layer depletion

CLIMATE CHANGE

This is a change in the climate pattern of a particular area. The most important cause of climate change is an elevation is greenhouse gases. These gases warm the atmosphere resulting in an increase in the average global temperature.

Image 1.6 A desert landscape

The Greenhouse effect

The greenhouse effect is very important in maintaining an average global temperature of about 15 degrees Celsius. Without the greenhouse effect, the average global temperature would be about -18 degree Celsius. This means the planet would be frozen all year round.

Image 1.7 A greenhouse used to grow plants by utilizing the greenhouse effect

Human activity results in the emission of high levels of green house gases into the atmosphere which cause a significant increase in the average global temperature. This is called global warming. The most important greenhouse gases are carbon dioxide, methane, water vapour and nitrous oxide.

Greenhouse Gases

Greenhouse Gases	Carbon Dioxide	Methane	Water Vapour	Nitrous Oxide
Sources	Fossil fuel	Agricultural activities, waste management	Water cycle	Fossil fuel, fertilizer use

Table 1.3 Greenhouse gases and their sources

How does the greenhouse effect work?

1. Sunlight penetrates the atmosphere.
2. The earth absorbs some of the radiation while the rest are reflected.
3. Greenhouse gases, present in the atmosphere, absorb some of the radiation.
4. This results in a higher surface temperature.

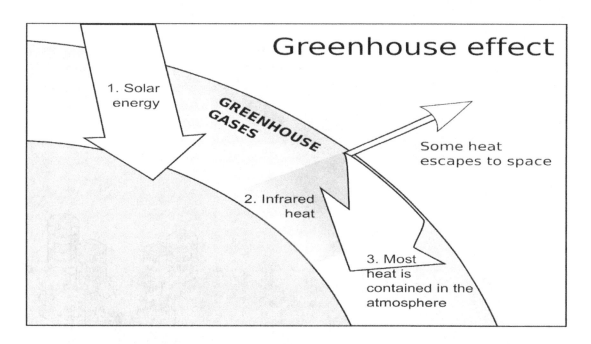

Figure 1.3 The greenhouse effect

POLLUTION

Pollution is the introduction of harmful substances into the natural environment. There are three main types of pollution: air pollution, water pollution and land pollution.

AIR POLLUTION

Air pollution occurs when excessive quantities of harmful substances are released into the atmosphere. This can be divided into natural and human causes.

Natural causes

Volcanic eruptions release large amounts of sulphur gases and carbon dioxide into the atmosphere.

Figure 1.4 A volcanic eruption

Wild fires burn large areas of forest, releasing carbon dioxide which contributes to global warming.

Image 1.8 Forest fire with a huge amount of smoke

Human Causes

The burning of fossil fuels result in the emission of green house gases which is the main cause of climate change.

Image 1.9 A large factory with gas emissions

Agricultural activities such as cattle farming releases high levels of methane that contributes to climate change.

Image 1.11 Dairy cattle produce methane in their faeces

Exhausts from cars and factories contain sulphur gases and nitrogen oxide which result in smog.

Toxic pollutants such as mercury, lead and benzene are released during the burning of coal and industrial waste.

Effects of air pollution

- Increased emission of greenhouse gases results in climate change which has a devastating effect on humans and the environment. This result in the melting of glaciers that leads to sea level rise. It also causes more frequent hurricanes, drought and coastal flooding.
- Urban smog can cause skin and lung problems.
- Toxic pollutants can lead to many types of cancers and other health problems.
- High levels of sulphur in the atmosphere results in acid rain which has a harmful effect on plants and aquatic animals.

How to prevent air pollution

- Air pollution can be reduced by limiting the use of fossil fuels. The use of renewable energy sources such as solar and hydroelectric power can significantly reduce air pollution.
- Better forest management can reduce wild fires especially in large forest such as the Amazon Rainforest.

WATER POLLUTION

Water pollution is the contamination of water bodies such as rivers and oceans by human activities.

Image 1.12 Plastic pollution of the ocean

What causes water pollution?

- Solid wastes such as plastics and sewage have a negative effect on aquatic life.

- Fertilizers and pesticides from agricultural activities contaminate underground water supply.

- Industrial wastes from factories can contaminate water supply resulting in the death of plants and animals.

- Oil spills from deep sea mines and large ships have a devastating effect on marine life.

Figure 1.5 Causes of water pollution

Effects of water pollution

- Water pollution can destroy marine habitat. Harmful chemicals such as lead, mercury and radioactive wastes can damage aquatic plant and animal life.

- Contaminated water can cause life threatening diseases such as cholera and gastroenteritis.

- Excess fertilizers in lakes can cause an overgrowth of algae which covers the water surface and blocks out sunlight. This results in the death of aquatic plants. Bacteria feeds off dead plants and use up all the oxygen. This results in the death of other organisms. This process is called eutrophication.

How to prevent water pollution

- Sewage should be properly treated before disposal into waterways.

- Great care must be taken to prevent the overuse of pesticides and fertilizers. This will prevent contamination of the nearby water sources.

- The use of biodegradable materials such as paper bags can replace plastics. This will help to reduce the amount of plastics in the oceans.

- Landfills and industrial waste sites should be positioned away from streams and underground water sources.

Image 1.13 Waste water treatment plant

LAND POLLUTION

Land pollution is the contamination or destruction of land by human activities.

What causes land pollution?

- The improper disposal of solid waste has a harmful effect on plants and animals.

Image 1.14 Overfull garbage bin

- Excess use of fertilizers and pesticides kill insects and other small animals that are vital to the ecosystem.

- Chemicals from factories can seep into to soil resulting in the death of plants and animals.

- Mining activities remove the top soil which is rich in nutrients. The soil that remains is not suitable for plant growth. Bauxite and limestone mining results in this type of land pollution.

Image 1.15 A limestone mine

- Deforestation is another form of land pollution. This results in soil erosion and the leaching of nutrients from the soil.

Effects of land pollution

- Habitat destruction results in the death of plants and animal species. Some species may only be found in that particular area and can become extinct.

- Land pollution can result in soil contamination that prevents its use for agricultural purposes. This can cause starvation and poverty.

- Harmful chemicals can enter the food chain and cause the death of humans and animals.

- Improper disposal of sewage can lead to health problems and even death.
- Chemicals from polluted land can be washed into rivers and streams causing water pollution.

How to prevent Land Pollution?

- Proper solid waste management is important in preventing land pollution. Wastes should be disposed of in designated areas.
- Farmers must be cautious when using fertilizers and pesticides.
- Industrial wastes should be properly disposed of.
- Forests should be regulated to prevent deforestation from mining, timber and agricultural activities.
- Reduce, recycle and reuse things as much as possible. This reduces the amount of solid wastes.
- Humans should develop and utilize more efficient farming methods such as aquaponics.

Figure 1.6 An aquaponics system uses a closed loop system to farm fish and vegetables.

DEFORESTATION

Deforestation is the permanent destruction of forests to make land available for other use. The land may be cleared to facilitate agricultural activities, housing development or for timber. This can have several harmful effects on the environment such as: loss of habitat, soil erosion and loss of biodiversity.

Image 1.16 Deforestation caused by logging

Forests play an integral role in climate change. Trees remove carbon dioxide from the atmosphere and release oxygen. Forests provide a home for millions of organisms, making them one of the most biodiverse ecosystems on earth. They are also a source of resources for humans. In addition, they provide raw materials for construction, medicine and clothing.

Forests can be protected by implementing strict regulations especially in large forests such as the Amazon Rainforest. Trees can be replanted to replace the ones that were removed. This is called reforestation.

OZONE DEPLETION

The ozone layer is a protective layer in the atmosphere that absorbs most of the sun's ultraviolet radiation. Human activities have resulted in the depletion of the ozone layer, creating a large hole over the South Pole. Chlorofluorocarbons (CFCs), found in aerosols, solvents and propellants, are responsible for most of the damage to the ozone layer. In 1989 the international community signed the Montreal Protocol which banned the production of CFCs. This has resulted in the progressive recovery of the ozone layer.

Figure 1.7 The ozone layer blocking sunlight

SOLID WASTE MANAGEMENT

Types of solid waste

- **Municipal Solid Waste (MSW)** - This refers to non-hazardous wastes such as: plastics, clothes and garbage.

Image 1.17 A garbage collection site

- **Hazardous Waste** - This refers to wastes that cause harm to humans and the environment for example: acids, gasoline and heavy metals.

Image 1.18 Hazardous waste

- **Industrial Waste** - This type of waste is more toxic and is produced from factories, for example, pharmaceutical waste.

- **Agricultural Waste** - This type of waste is generated from crops and farm animals, for example, animal dung.

- **Bio-Medical Waste** - This type of waste is produced from hospitals, clinics and research institutions, for example, human tissue and body fluids.

The National Solid Waste Management Authority (NSWMA) is a government organization responsible for the collection and disposal of solid wastes in Jamaica.

Solid Waste Management Process

Figure 1.8 Methods of garbage disposal

1. **Waste generation:** This includes any activities involved in identifying materials that are no longer usable.

2. **Onsite storage:** This relates to activities at the point of waste generation, which facilitate easier collection. For example, waste bins.

3. **Waste collection and transportation:** This involves the collection and transportation of wastes from the waste generation site to the disposal site.

4. **Waste processing:** This refers to the sorting of wastes to separate materials that can be recycled from unusable materials.

5. **Disposal:** The final stage of waste management. It involves the activities aimed at the systematic disposal of waste materials in locations such as landfills or waste-to-energy facilities.

Types of waste disposal

1. Landfill
2. Incineration
3. Deep burial
4. Chemical treatment

Landfill

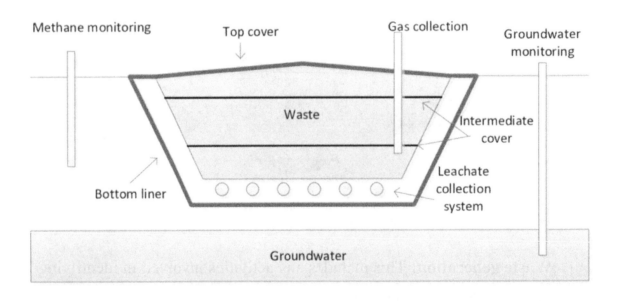

Figure 1.9 A diagram of a landfill layout

ADAPTATIONS OF ORGANISMS TO THEIR ENVIRONMENT

Adaptations are inheritable characteristics that increase an organism's ability to survive and reproduce in an environment. Organisms from different environments develop unique characteristics that are specifically suited for that environment. Adaptations can be physical or behavioral. An example of physical adaption is how giraffes develop long necks to reach food in tall trees. An example of behavioral adaptation is how emperor penguins in Antarctica crowd together to keep warm during the winter.

Polar bears live in very cold environment. They have a thick fur that keeps them warm during the winter.

Image 1.19 A pair of polar bears

Kangaroo rats can survive without drinking water. They get all the water they need from the seeds they eat. This allows them to survive in the desert.

Image 1.20 A kangaroo rat

Cuttlefish creates exceptional camouflage to hide from predators.

Image 1.21 A picture of a cuttlefish

Cactus stores water in the leaves enabling it to survive in the desert.

Image 1.22 Cactus in a desert

END OF TOPIC TEST

1. Write an essay to your Member of Parliament, discussing the causes of water pollution in your area. Discuss the causes and effects on the environment and outline some solutions.

_____

_____

_____

_____

_____

2. Explain the causes of climate change.

3. Explain the effects of land pollution on the environment.

_____

_____

_____

_____

_____

_____

_____

4. Outline the causes of air pollution.

_____

_____

_____

_____

_____

_____

_____

5. With the aid of a diagram, explain the greenhouse effect.

_____

_____

_____

_____

_____

_____

_____

6. Discuss the methods of waste disposal used in Jamaica.

_____

_____

_____

_____

_____

_____

_____

7. A new bauxite company wants to mine bauxite in your community. Explain how this will affect the environment.

_____

_____

_____

8. The government wants to create a new environment policy. Write a letter to the minister outlining methods of conserving the environment.

_____
_____
_____
_____
_____
_____
_____
_____
_____
_____
_____
_____
_____
_____
_____
_____
_____
_____

9. Using examples, explain how animals adapt to their environment.

_____
_____
_____

_____

_____

_____

_____

_____

10. Identify the sources of greenhouse gases.

_____

_____

_____

_____

_____

_____

_____

_____

_____

_____

CHAPTER 2: LIGHT AND SOUND

LIGHT

Light is a form of energy that allows us to visually perceive the environment. Without light, everything would be totally black. A lot of things that we enjoy such as watching television would not be possible without light. Light is considered as both a particle and a wave. The smallest particle of light is called a photon. When light is produced it travels in a straight line in all directions. This is called radiation.

Figure 2.1 The sun producing light

Speed of light

Light travels in a straight line at a speed of approximately 300,000 km/sec. The sun is about 150,000,000 km from the earth. It takes only eight minutes and twenty seconds for light from the sun to reach the earth.

SOURCES OF LIGHT

Luminous Objects

Luminous objects are objects that produce their own light, for example, light bulb, the sun, flashlight, fire, etc.

Figure 2.2 A light bulb

Non-luminous objects

Non-luminous objects do not produce their own light, for example, table, tree, rock, the moon, etc. The moon is non-luminous because it does not produce its own light. The moon is actually a huge ball of rock. It looks bright in the sky because it is reflecting the light from the sun.

Image 2.1 The moon

35

TRANSMISSION OF LIGHT

Transparent objects

Transparent objects allow light to pass through. Examples of transparent objects include: water, air, glass, etc.

Transparent Object

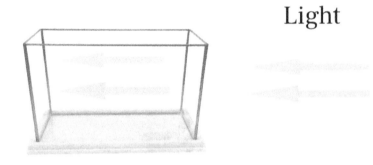

Figure 2.3 A transparent glass box

Translucent objects

Translucent objects allow some light to pass through. They are referred to as semi-transparent. Examples include: coloured glass, tinted window and sunglasses.

Translucent Object

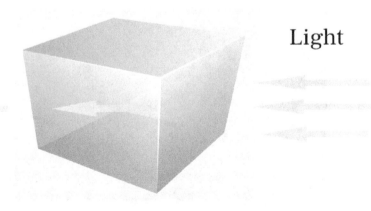

Figure 2.4 A translucent cube

Opaque objects

Opaque objects do not allow light to pass through. Examples of opaque objects include: wood, wall and cell phones.

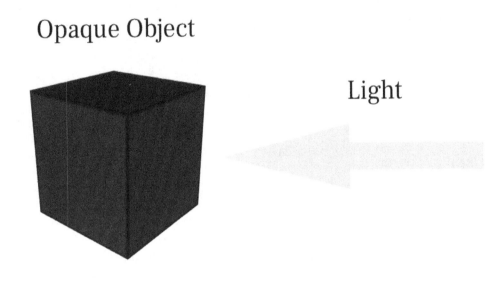

Figure 2.5 An opaque cube

HOW LIGHT HELPS US TO SEE

Our eyes allow us the see everything around us. They receive information from the environment and send it to the brain where it is interpreted. When light is produced, it travels through the cornea and the pupil to the lens. The lens bends (refracts) the light to focus it on the retina. The image is formed upside down on the retina. The retina then sends the information to the brain via the optic nerve. The brain interprets the image as upright.

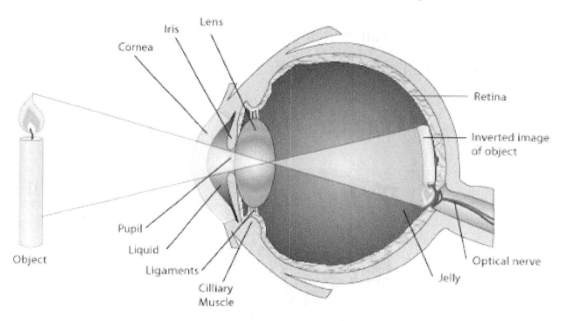

Figure 2.6 A diagram of the eye showing the transmission of light

Reflection of light

Reflection is the bending of light when it comes into contact with a smooth shiny surface, for example, glass and shiny metals. The light rays are reflected at the same angle as they hit the surface. A mirror is a great example of light reflection.

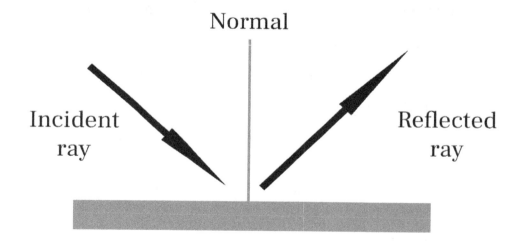

Figure 2.7 Reflection of light from a mirror

Refraction of light

Refraction is the bending of light when it passes from one medium to another. This bending of light occurs because light travels at different speed in different medium. Examples include: lenses that are used in glasses to improve vision.

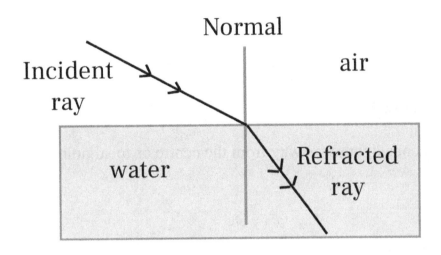

Figure 2.8 Refraction of light when light travels from air into water

Lens

A lens is a transparent object with two curved surfaces that is able to bend light. They are usually made of glass or plastic and are commonly used in eyeglasses and cameras. There are two types of lenses:

- Concave lens
- Convex lens

Convex or Converging lens

These lenses are elliptical is shape and are used to bend light inwards towards a focal point.

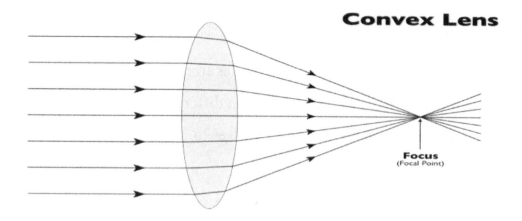

Figure 2.9 A convex lens bending light inwards

Concave or Diverging lens

This type of lens bends light rays away from the centre or focal point.

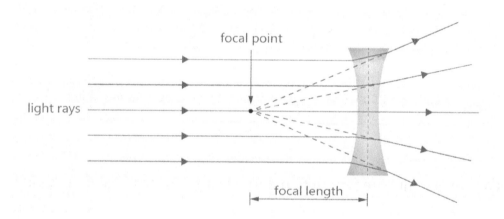

Figure 2.11 A concave lens bending light outwards

Science Experiment- Bending of light

In this experiment we will assess the refraction of light.

Procedure:

1. *Place a pencil in a glass and put the glass on a flat surface.*
2. *Half fill the glass with water.*
3. *Observe and record your findings.*

Figure 2.12 A pencil in a beaker of water

Discuss the results.

_____

_____

_____

_____

_____

_____

_____

_____

Colours of white light

White light consists of a spectrum of different colours. When white light passes through a prism the spectrum of colours can be observed. The colours are arranged in a specific order: red, orange, yellow, green, blue and violet. This can be seen when sunlight passes through water droplets and forms a rainbow.

SOUND

Sound is a rapid vibration of particles that produces an audible wave in a medium such as a solid, liquid or gas. Energy is required to produce a sound, for example, a speaker uses electrical energy to produce a sound. Hitting a metal with a stick causes the particles to vibrate in a wave form and produce a sound. The speed of sound in air is 344 m/s.

Frequency or Pitch

The frequency or pitch of a sound refers to the number of vibration per second. The frequency is measured in hertz (Hz). Low frequency vibrations produce low pitch sound, while high frequency vibrations produce high pitch sounds. Humans are able to hear sound between 20 Hz and 20,000 Hz. Dogs are able to hear sounds up to 40,000 Hz. Any sound with a frequency below 20 Hz is known as an infrasound and any sound with a frequency above 20,000 Hz is known as an ultrasound.

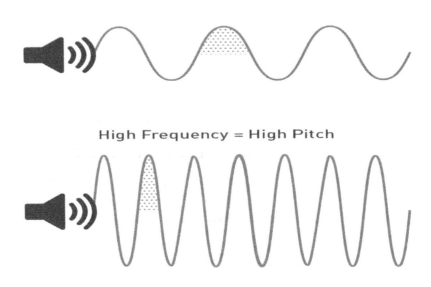

Figure 2.13 the frequency of sound wave

Science Experiment- Pitch

In this experiment we will examine the pitch of a sound.

Procedure:

1. Secure one end of a plastic ruler to the edge of a table and allow the other end to hang over the edge.
2. Measure the length of ruler over the edge.
3. Pluck the free end of the ruler and record your findings.
4. Repeat the procedure three times with different ruler lengths.
5. Record your findings.

Length	High speed	Medium speed	Slow speed	High pitch	Medium pitch	Low pitch

Table 2.1 Results of the sound experiment

Discuss the results.

_____

_____

_____

_____

_____

_____

Amplitude or Loudness

The amplitude refers to the size of the vibration. Large vibrations produce louder sounds while smaller vibrations produce softer sounds. When you whisper, the vocal cords produce small vibrations in the air resulting in a soft sound. Shouting cause the vocal cords to vibrate more vigorously producing a louder sound.

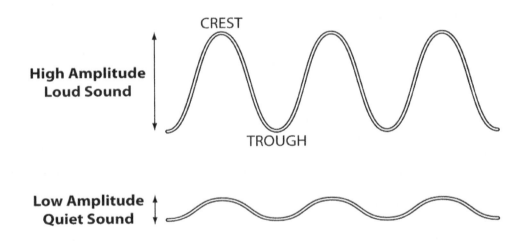

Figure 2.14 Sound waves showing the amplitude of loud and soft sound

Reflection of Sound

The bouncing back of sound from a solid surface is called reflection. The reflected sound is called an echo. This can be heard when you shout in a large empty room. The sound bounces off the walls and reach the ears at a later time than when the sound was produced.

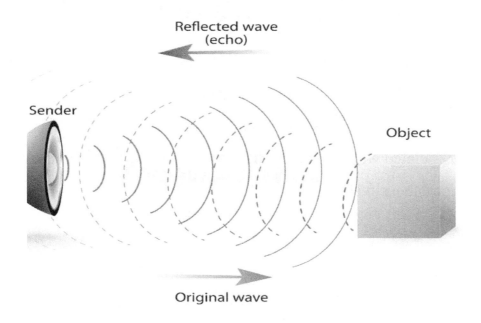

Figure 2.15 Echo

Animals such as dolphins and bats use echoes to perceive their environment. These animals produce a sound that gets reflected. This allows them to move around in the dark.

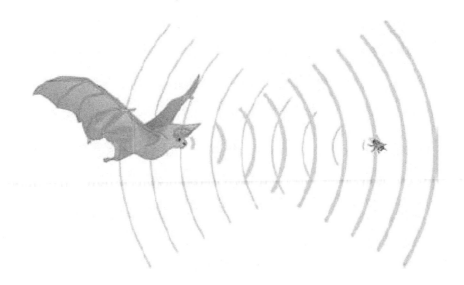

Figure 2.16 A bat using echolocation to locate prey

NOISE POLLUTION

This refers to the harmful effects of loud sounds on humans and animals. Some causes of noise pollution include: industrial machines, loud music, transportation, construction and explosions. Noise pollution can have devastating effects on humans. It is associated with permanent hearing loss, cardiovascular disease and psychological problems in children.

Figure 2.17 Noise pollution

Noise pollution can be reduced by proper urban planning. Residential areas should not be close to industrial areas. Laws can be established to prevent the playing of loud music in residential areas. If you have to be around noise, you can protect your ears with ear plugs or ear muffs.

END OF TOPIC TEST

1. Discuss the importance of light to humans.

   _____

   _____

   _____

   _____

   _____

   _____

   _____

2. Explain the difference between luminous and non-luminous objects.

   _____

   _____

   _____

   _____

   _____

   _____

   _____

3. The moon appears bright in the night sky. Is the moon a luminous or non-luminous object? Explain your answer.

   _____

   _____

   _____

   _____

   _____

_____

_____

4. Explain why you are able to see yourself when you look in a mirror.

_____

_____

_____

_____

_____

_____

5. A rainbow appeared after a brief shower of rain. Explain how a rainbow is formed.

_____

_____

_____

_____

_____

_____

_____

6. A pencil is placed in a glass of water. On observation, the pencil appears to be bent. Explain your observation.

7. Explain how sound travels through a medium.

8. Explain the difference between frequency and amplitude of a sound.

9. Explain how dolphins use sound to communicate with the environment.

_____

_____

_____

_____

_____

_____

_____

_____

10. Discuss the causes and effects of noise pollution in your community.

_____

_____

_____

_____

_____

_____

_____

_____

CHAPTER 3: MATERIALS

Materials are the building blocks of every civilization. From stone and wood to concrete and steel, humans have manipulated different materials over the centuries. Materials are useful for particular purposes because they have specific qualities, which are referred to as properties. Understanding the properties of materials helps us to determine the usefulness of the materials available to us.

Image 3.1 Plastic, gravel, wood, steel, concrete and rubber

Properties of materials

1. **Hardness:** Resistance to scratching and pressure. Hardwood does not get marked as easily as softwood.

2. **Strength:** Amount of force needed to break a material usually by pushing or pulling.

3. **Toughness:** Resistance to breaking by cracking, opposite to 'brittle'.

4. **Stiffness:** Amount of force needed to change the shape of a material, opposite to flexible.

5. **Elasticity:** Ability to return to its original shape when a force is removed, for example, rubber band.

6. **Plasticity:** Ability to retain the new shape when a force is removed, for example, metals.

7. **Absorbency:** Ability of a material to soak up a liquid.

8. **Waterproof:** Resistance to liquids; repels water.

9. **Flexibility:** Ability of an object to bend or deform in response to an applied force.

10. **Durability:** Ability to withstand wear, pressure, or damage; hard-wearing.

11. **Magnetic Property:** This refers to the ability of a material to be influenced by a magnetic field.

12. **Transparency:** The ability of a material to allow light to pass through it.

13. **Heat Conductivity:** The ability of a material to transmit heat.

14. **Electrical conductivity:** The ability of a material to transmit electricity.

Science Experiment- Material properties

In this experiment we will compare the properties of different materials.

Procedure:

1. *Get a piece of wood, elastic band, a piece of plastic and a piece of metal.*

2. ***Test for magnetism:*** *Place a magnet close to each item and record your observations.*

3. **Test for strength:** *Try to bend each item with the same amount of force. Record your findings.*

4. **Test for elasticity:** *Stretch each item with the same amount of force.*

5. **Heat conductivity:** *Place each item close to a lit candle for 5 minutes. Use a thermometer to measure the temperature of the side away from the flame. Record your findings.*

Complete this table with the results.

Materials	Magnetic	Strength	Elasticity	Heat conductivity
Wood				
Elastic Band				
Plastic				
Metal				

Table 3.1 Results of the material properties experiment

Discuss the results.

_____

_____

_____

_____

_____

_____

MATERIALS AND THEIR PROPERTIES

METAL	
Properties	**Uses**
Strong	Bridges
Shiny	Cars
Conducts heat and electricity	Pots
Some are magnetic	Electrical wires

Table 3.2 Properties of metals

PLASTIC	
Properties	**Uses**
Soft	Bottles
Waterproof	Pipes
Flexible	Containers
Durable	Bags
Lightweight	Television

Table 3.3 Properties of plastics

WOOD	
Properties	**Uses**
Hard	Houses
Durable	Furniture
Poor Conductor	Paper
Non-Flexible	Tools

Table 3.4 Properties of wood

GLASS	
Properties	**Uses**
Transparent	Mirrors
Heat Resistant	Windshields in cars
Chemical Resistant	Drinking glass
Brittle	Greenhouse

Table 3.5 Properties of glass

IRREVERSIBLE CHANGES

A change is called irreversible if it cannot be changed back again. In an irreversible change, new materials are always formed. Irreversible changes are permanent. They cannot be undone. For example, you cannot change a cake back into its ingredients.

Types of irreversible changes

Heating

Heating can cause an irreversible change. For example, you heat a raw egg to cook it. The cooked egg cannot be changed back to a raw egg.

Mixing

Mixing substances can cause an irreversible change. For example, when vinegar and bicarbonate of soda are mixed, the mixture changes and lots of bubbles of carbon dioxide are made. The new liquid cannot be turned back into vinegar and bicarbonate of soda.

Burning

Burning is an example of an irreversible change. When you burn wood you get ash and smoke. You cannot change the ash and smoke back to wood.

REVERSIBLE CHANGES

A reversible change is a change that can be undone or reversed. A reversible change might change how a material looks or feels, but it does not create new materials. Examples of reversible changes include: dissolving, evaporation, melting and freezing.

STATES OF MATTER

Matter is anything that has mass and occupies space. Matter can exist as solids, liquids or gases and can change state depending on the temperature of the material.

Properties of Solids

1. Retains a fixed volume and shape
2. Rigid - particles locked into place
3. Not easily compressible
4. Little free space between particles
5. Does not flow easily
6. Particles cannot move or slide past one another

SOLID

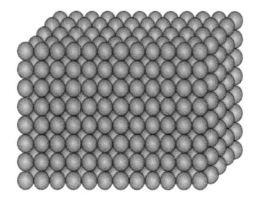

Figure 3.1 The arrangement of particles in a solid

Properties of Liquid

1. Assumes the shape of the part of the container which it occupies

2. Particles can move or slide past one another

3. Not easily compressible

4. Little free space between particles

5. Flows easily

LIQUID

Figure 3.2 The arrangement of particles in a liquid

Properties of Gas

1. Assumes the shape of the part of the container which it occupies

2. Particles can move past one another

3. Easily compressible

4. Lots of free space between particles

5. Flows easily

GAS

 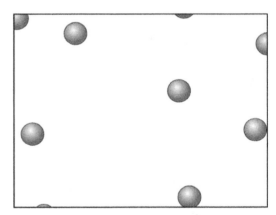

Figure 3.3 The arrangement of particles in a gas

CHANGING STATE

Melting point: This is the point at which a solid becomes a liquid.

Boiling point: This is the point at which a liquid becomes a gas.

Freezing point: This is the point at which a liquid becomes a solid.

STATE CHANGE

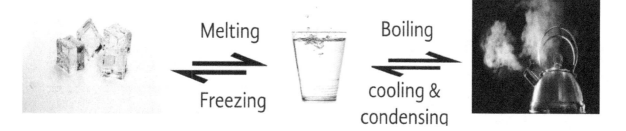

Figure 3.4 Changing state between solid, liquid and gas

Material	Boiling (°C) Becomes a gas	Freezing (°C) Becomes a solid	Melting (°C) Becomes a liquid
Water	100° C	0° C	0° C
Iron	2750° C	1535° C	1535° C
Ethyl Alcohol	78° C	-114° C	-114° C

Table 3.6 The boiling, melting and freezing points for different substances

END OF TOPIC TEST

1. Identify three (3) materials and state one use of each.

_____

_____

_____

_____

_____

_____

_____

_____

_____

2. List and explain three (3) material properties.

_____

_____

_____

_____

_____

_____

_____

_____

3. With the aid of a diagram, explain the three (3) states of matter.

_____

_____

_____

_____

_____

_____

_____

_____

4. Explain the properties of solids, liquids and gases.

_____

_____

_____

_____

_____

_____

_____

_____

_____

5. With the use of an example, explain what is meant by boiling point.

_____

_____

_____

_____

_____

_____

_____

_____

6. With the aid of an example, explain melting point.

_____

_____

_____

_____

_____

_____

_____

_____

7. Explain how a solid becomes a gas.

_____

_____

_____

_____

_____

_____

_____

_____

_____

8. Explain why plastics are one of the most widely used materials.

_____

_____

_____

_____

_____

_____

_____

_____

9. Explain the difference between reversible and irreversible change.

_____

_____

_____

_____

_____

_____

_____

CHAPTER 4: ORGAN SYSTEMS

The human body consists of different organs that work together as a single unit. This is called an organ system.

THE DIGESTIVE SYSTEM

The digestive system consists of a group of organs that work together to break down food into smaller components that can be absorbed and used by the body. Digestion begins in the mouth and ends at the anus. The digestive system consists of the alimentary canal or gastrointestinal tract, liver and pancreas. The gastrointestinal track includes the mouth, oesophagus, stomach, small intestine, large intestine, rectum and anus. As food moves through the gastrointestinal tract several changes occur.

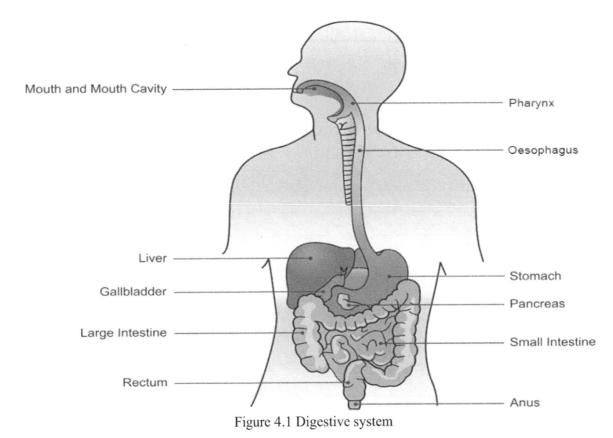

Figure 4.1 Digestive system

The Mouth

Digestion of food begins in the mouth. Food taken in the mouth is broken down by the teeth into smaller pieces. It is also mixed with saliva which is produced by the salivary glands in the mouth. The saliva consists of digestive juices that help to break down the food. The tongue helps to mix the food with the saliva and forms a ball of food called a bolus. The bolus is pushed to the back of the mouth and is swallowed.

The Oesophagus

The oesophagus or gullet is a long muscular tube that connects the mouth to the stomach. It transports the bolus of food from the mouth and empties it into the stomach. It does not produce any digestive juice but the digestive juices from the saliva continue to break down the food as it passes through the oesophagus.

The Stomach

The stomach is a muscular sac that temporarily stores food until it is small enough to pass into the small intestine. The stomach produces a strong acid that helps to break down food as well as kills bacteria that was swallowed with the food. The muscular walls of the stomach push the food around, breaking it up into much smaller pieces. The stomach produces digestive juices that contain enzymes that further break down the food. The food is then passed into the small intestine.

Small Intestine

The small intestine is the main site for digestion and adsorption. Partially digested food from the stomach, enters the small intestine and is mixed with digestive juice from the liver, pancreas and walls of the small intestine. The food is broken down into tiny components that are absorbed into the blood stream.

The small intestine is divided into three parts; duodenum, jejunum and ileum.

1. The Duodenum is the first and shortest segment of the small intestine. The pancreas, liver and gallbladder release chemicals into the duodenum that breaks down the food.
2. The Jejunum is the middle segment of the small intestine found between the duodenum and ileum. This segment is responsible for digestion and absorption.
3. The ileum is the final and longest segment of the small intestine that connects to the large intestine. It is responsible for the absorption of digested food.

The Liver and Pancreas

These are solid organs that produce digestive juices that help to break down food. The liver produces bile which is stored in the gallbladder. Bile is released into the small intestine to assist with digestion. The pancreas is a flat organ that releases enzymes directly into the small intestines. These enzymes play a very important role in the final stages of digestion.

The Large Intestine

Waste material from the small intestine enters into the large intestine. No enzymes are produced in the large intestine. The walls of the large intestine absorb excess water from the undigested material. This material is then passed into the rectum where it is stored and excreted through the anus.

The Rectum

This is an 8-inches long chamber that connects the large intestine to the anus. The role of the rectum is to store the waste materials left over from the digested food.

The left-over materials are called "stool". When the stool comes into the rectum, sensory cells send a message to the brain. The brain then decides if the stool can be released or not.

The Anus

This is the last part of the digestive tract. The anus controls the release of stool.

THE RESPIRATORY SYSTEM

This is the system of the human body that is responsible for the intake of oxygen and expelling carbon dioxide. It is what enables us to breathe. During breathing, we inhale the oxygen from the air and exhale carbon dioxide produced in our body. Our body needs oxygen to survive.

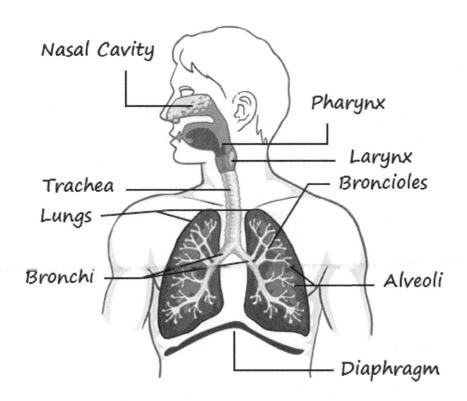

Figure 4.2 Respiratory system

The respiratory system is divided into two sections, the lower and upper respiratory tract.

THE UPPER RESPIRATORY TRACT

This includes: the nose, mouth and the pharynx.

The Nose

This is where the air enters the body. Inside the nose there are tiny hairs called cilia which filter, humidify or moisten and warm or cool the air before it enters the lungs. The cilia are said to protect our bodies from about 20 billion particles daily.

The mouth

The main functions of the mouth are eating and communication. However, it can also be used to breathe. The air enters through your mouth in order to be passed down to the lungs.

Pharynx

This is an area at the back of the throat that connects the nose and mouth to the trachea.

THE LOWER RESPIRATORY TRACT

This section is where the breathing takes place. It consists of the trachea, bronchi, and the lungs.

The Trachea or Windpipe

It is responsible for transporting the air to your lungs. It is an average of 4 inches long and lined with mucus that traps unwanted particles before they can enter the lungs. The trachea begins just under the larynx (voice box) and runs down behind the breastbone (sternum). The trachea then divides into two smaller tubes called bronchi;

The Bronchi

These are two hollow tubes that connect the trachea to the lungs. One bronchus takes air to the left lung while the other takes air to the right lung. Inside the lung the bronchi divide into smaller tubes called broncheoli that end at the alveoli.

The Lungs

It is a pair of organs found in all vertebrates (animals with backbone). There are two lungs, the left lung and the right lung. Inside the lungs are the bronchial tree which are air tubes that branches off into smaller and smaller tubes, each ending in a pulmonary alveolus. The pulmonary alveoli are small air spaces inside your lungs that allows for oxygen to enter the blood and carbon dioxide to leave.

THE PROCESS OF BREATHING

There are two stages in this process: Exhaling and Inhaling.

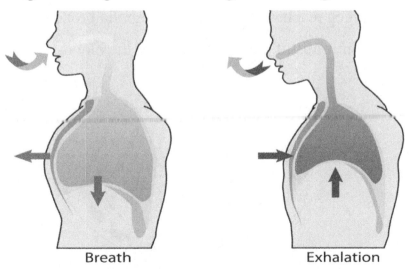

Breath   Exhalation

Figure 4.3 Movement of the chest during breathing

Inhaling

This is the intake of air into the lungs through the nose and mouth, which causes the lungs to expand.

The air passes through the mucus lined windpipe, where unwanted particles get trapped. The rib muscles contracts, causing the ribs to rise and increases the chest volume. As the chest cavity expands, it reduces the air pressure and caused the air to be drawn into the lungs. The diaphragm flattens to further increase the chest volume. The oxygen from the air enters into the bloodstream and is circulated through the body.

Exhaling

The chest wall muscles relax and the diaphragm curves upwards. These actions decrease the chest volume and increase the pressure inside the chest. This forces air, that is rich in carbon dioxide, out of the lungs. The air travels up through the trachea and is exhaled through the nose or mouth.

Gas Exchange

Gas exchange occurs inside the alveoli. These are small air sacs with very thin walls. Air rich in oxygen reaches the alveoli through the bronchial system. The oxygen crosses the thin walls of the alveoli to enter the blood.

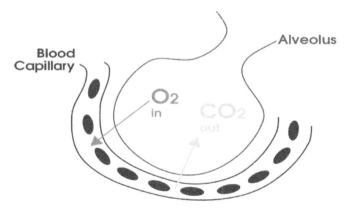

Figure 4.4 Gaseous exchange in the alveoli

The body tissues use oxygen from the blood in order to carry out their function. This causes the oxygen level in the blood to fall and the level of carbon dioxide to increase. The carbon dioxide rich blood, travels to the lungs where carbon dioxide leaves the blood.

THE CIRCULATORY SYSTEM

The circulatory system or cardiovascular system is a large network of organs and blood vessels. This network supplies tissues in the body with oxygen and nutrients, transport hormones and removes unnecessary waste products. Nutrients, oxygen and hormones are delivered to every cell in the body and waste products such as carbon dioxide are removed. The circulatory system helps to fight off diseases and assist in maintaining a normal body temperature.

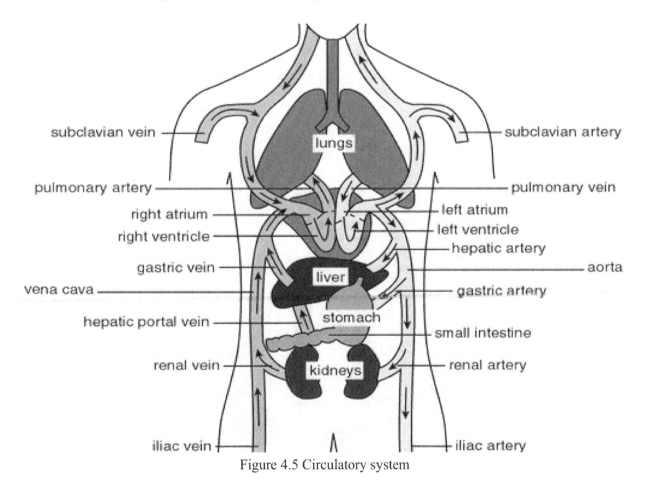

Figure 4.5 Circulatory system

The circulatory system not only keeps the body healthy, but it keeps the body alive. The rest of the body sends signals to the heart, which tells the heart how hard to pump in order to properly supply the body with what it needs. When you sleep, the body sends electrical signals to the heart, instructing it to slow down. When you are exercising, the heart receives messages to pump harder in order to supply the body with extra oxygen for the muscles.

THE PARTS OF THE CIRCULATORY SYSTEM

The Heart

The heart is a muscular organ that is about the size of your closed fist. It is in the left centre of your chest. The heart beats about 70 times per minute or about 100,000 times daily. It is divided into a right and left side by a septum. The blood from either side does not mix. The right side of the heart pumps blood that is low in oxygen (deoxygenated) and the left side of the heart pumps blood that is rich in oxygen (oxygenated).

The human heart has four chambers. Flap-like valves, present between the chambers, prevents blood from flowing backwards.

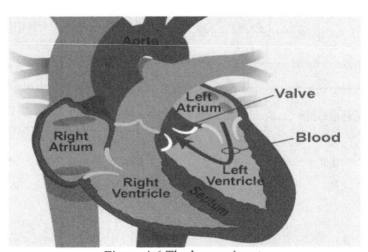

Figure 4.6 The human heart

- **Right atrium**- This chamber receives deoxygenated blood from the body and pumps it into the right ventricle.

- **Right ventricle**- This chamber pumps deoxygenated blood to the lungs where it becomes oxygenated.

- **Left atrium** – This chamber receives oxygenated blood from the lungs and pumps it to the left ventricle.

- **Left ventricle**- This chamber has the thickest muscles as it pumps oxygenated blood to the entire body.

Artery

These are large thick walled blood vessels that take blood from the heart to the rest of the body. They contain blood that is rich in oxygen (oxygenated blood). You can differentiate a vein from an artery by feeling for a pulse. Only arteries have a pulse.

Veins

These are thin walled blood vessels that take blood from the tissues to the heart. Veins contain deoxygenated blood (blood that is low in oxygen).

Capillary

These are very tiny blood vessels that connect veins to arteries. The small vessels slow down the blood flow which gives the tissues enough time the extract the oxygen and nutrients they need.

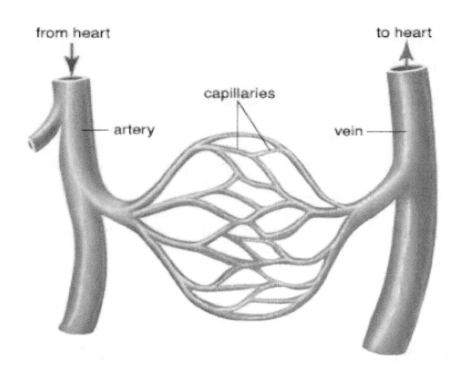

from heart

to heart

capillaries

artery

vein

Figure 4.7 Artery capillary and vein

The Blood

This is a fluid that transports oxygen and nutrients to cells in the body and carries carbon dioxide and other waste products away from the tissues. The average human being has about 5 liters of blood that is constantly pumped around the body. The blood is made up of three main components:

- **Red blood cells** - These cells are responsible for transporting oxygen around the body. This is what gives the blood its red colour.
- **White blood cells** - These cells act as the soldiers of the body. They protect the body by finding and killing harmful substances such as a virus or bacteria.
- **Plasma (fluid)** - This is the liquid part of the blood. It transports useful substances such as nutrients to the cells and removes waste such are carbon dioxide.

THE MOVEMENT OF BLOOD THROUGH THE BODY

1. Deoxygenated blood from the tissues travel to the right side of the heart through large veins.

2. The blood enters the right atrium which pumps it to the right ventricle.

3. The right ventricle pumps the deoxygenated blood to the lungs where it becomes oxygenated.

4. The oxygenated blood travels to the left atrium which pumps it to the left ventricle.

5. The left ventricles then pump the oxygenated blood to the tissues.

6. The tissues use up the oxygen in the blood and produces deoxygenated blood. The deoxygenated blood travels back to the heart.

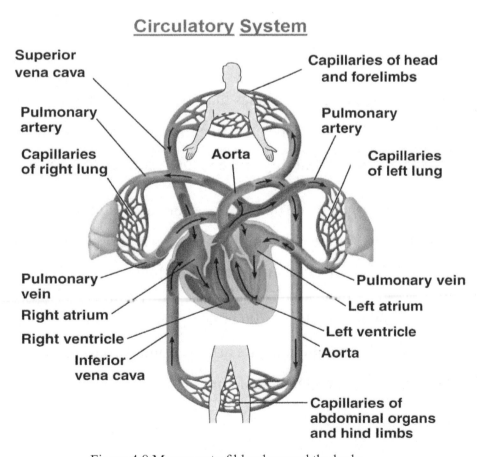

Figure 4.8 Movement of blood around the body

THE MUSCULOSKELETAL SYSTEM

SKELETAL SYSTEM

The skeletal system consists of all the bones and joints in the human body. The most important functions of the skeletal system are:

- Supporting the body
- Produces blood cells
- Facilitates movement
- Protects internal organs
- Stores and releases minerals and fat

Supporting the body means that the bones supports the body's weight. Without the skeletal system, your body would be a lump of mass, organs, muscles and skin. The skeletal system is composed of bones and cartilage.

Bones are hard, dense connective tissues that form most of the skeletal system. In sections of the body where the bones move, cartilage which is a semi-rigid form of connective tissue provides flexibility and a smooth surface for movement.

Each bone is a living organ made up of cells, proteins and minerals. Our skeletal system provides points for attachment of muscles that allows the joints to move. Additionally, the bone marrow produces blood cells.

The human body contains a total of 206 bones. The skull consists of 22 separate bones. The bones in the human body are arranged into two divisions called the axial skeleton and the appendicular skeleton.

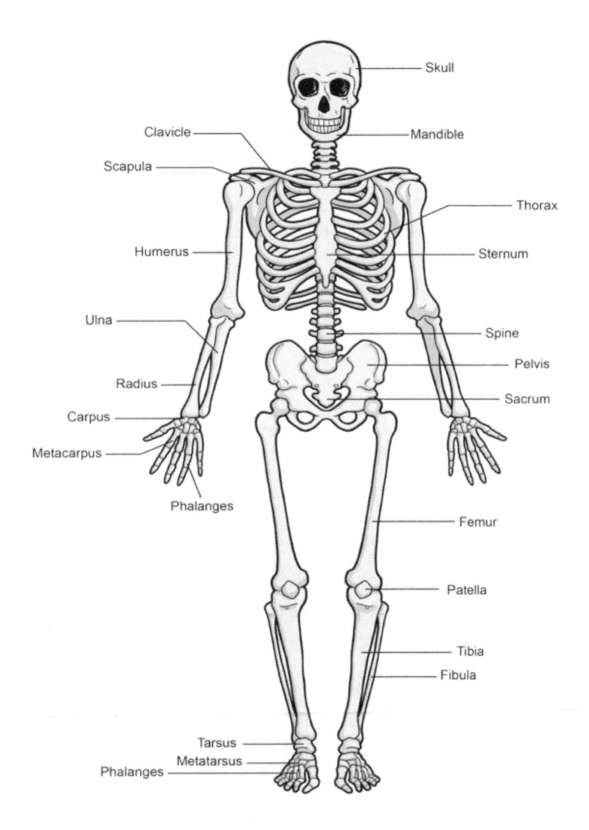

Figure 4.9 Skeletal system

The axial skeleton runs through the middle of the body. This includes:

- The skull
- Vertebral Column
- Ribs
- Sternum

The appendicular skeleton is made of 120 bones in the regions listed below:

- The upper limbs
- Lower limbs
- Pelvic girdle
- Shoulders

THE MUSCULAR SYSTEM

This system is responsible for the movement, posture and balance of the human body. They are attached to and work with the bones of the skeletal system in order to facilitate movement. There are about 700 named muscles in the human body which make up most of your body weight. Muscles are also found in organs such as the heart and inside of some digestive organs.

Skeletal muscles are voluntary muscles in the human body. This means that you can consciously control them. These muscles allow every physical action that a person performs, such as speaking, running and writing. The function of the skeletal muscle is to contract in order to move parts of the body.

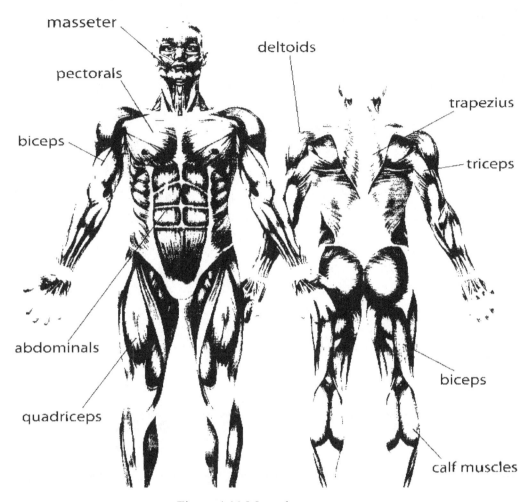

masseter

deltoids

pectorals

trapezius

biceps

triceps

abdominals

biceps

quadriceps

calf muscles

Figure 4.11 Muscular system

Movement

Skeletal muscles are usually attached to two bones across a joint. When the muscle contracts it pulls on the bone across the joint. This causes the joint to bend, extend or twist. The type of movement is determined by the position of attachment.

The biceps are attached to the shoulder bones and to the forearm bones. It crosses the elbow joint. When the biceps contract they pull on the forearm bones causing the elbow to bend.

Let us review an example using the elbow joint.

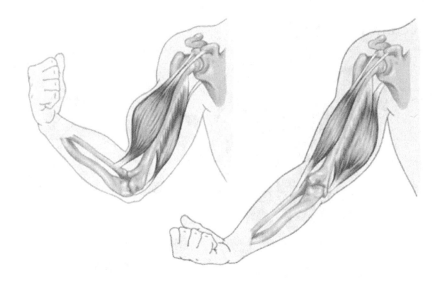

Figure 4.12 Movement at the elbow joint

THE NERVOUS SYSTEM

The nervous system is a group of nerves and special cells called neurons that sends signals between parts of our body. It is the electrical wiring of the human body. It is also the controlling, regulatory and communicating system of the body. All mental activity occurs here, including your thoughts, learning and memory. The nervous system works with the endocrine system to maintain a stable, balanced and constant environment in the body.

The nervous system is divided into two main parts:

- Central nervous system
- Peripheral nervous system

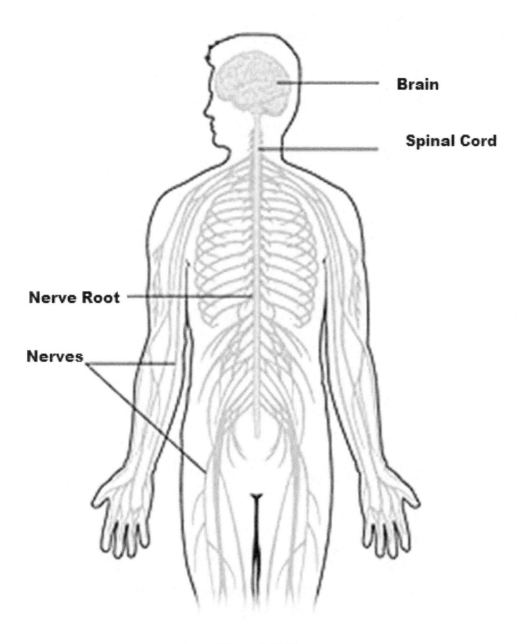

Figure 4.13 Nervous system

CENTRAL NERVOUS SYSTEM

The central nervous system controls most functions of the body. It consists of the brain and the spinal cord.

The brain

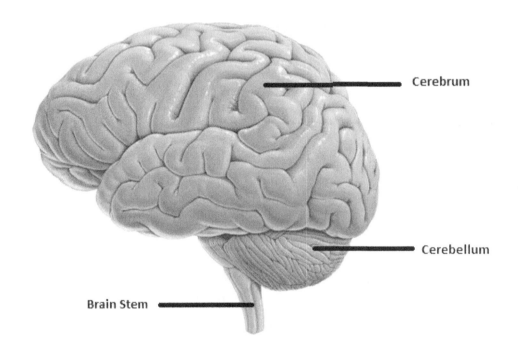

Figure 4.14 Brain

The brain is the most complex organ in the human body. It controls our thoughts, body functions and interprets our environment. Nerves from all parts of the body send signals to the brain. The brain analyzes this information and sends out an appropriate response. For example, Andrew is standing in the middle of the road when a car was approaching. He saw the car and got out of the way. Let us review how he was able to do this:

1. His eyes sent a signal to his brain.
2. His brain interpreted the signal and recognized that he was in danger.
3. The brain sent a signal to his leg muscles instructing them to contract.

4. The leg muscles contract and he walks out of danger.

The brain has three main parts:

- **Cerebrum-** This is the largest part of the brain. This area controls all our thoughts, reasoning and other involuntary functions. This area determines our personality.
- **Cerebellum-** This is located at the base of the brain and is responsible for balance and coordination.
- **Brain Stem-** This area connects the brain to the spinal cord. This area controls our heart rate and breathing.

The Spinal Cord

This is the connection between the body and the brain. It allows the brain to communicate with the body. The spinal cord receives signals from the body and sends them to the brain where they are analyzed and relayed back through the spinal cord. If the spinal cord gets damaged or injured, the communication between the brain and the rest of the body would be affected.

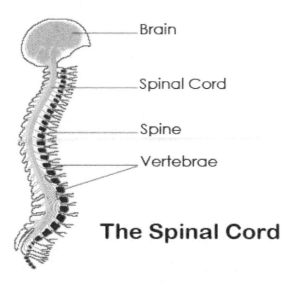

Figure 4.15 Spinal cord

The spinal cord is protected by the spinal column which extends from the base of the skull down the centre of the back.

The spinal cord allows the body to:

- Move
- Feel hot and cold temperature, vibrations, sharp and dull sensations
- Sense the position of your arms and legs
- Controls bodily functions such as breathings, urination and bowel movements.

Reflex Arc

A reflex arc is an involuntary action that occurs without any input from the brain. For example, if you accidentally touch a hot pot, you quickly pull away your finger.

1. The heat from the pot sends a signal to the spinal cord along a special nerve called a sensory nerve.
2. In the spinal cord, the sensory nerve passes the information to the relay nerve.
3. The relay nerve sends a response to the muscles in the arm via an effector nerve.
4. This allows you to quickly pull away your hand to minimize the damage.

Reflex Arc

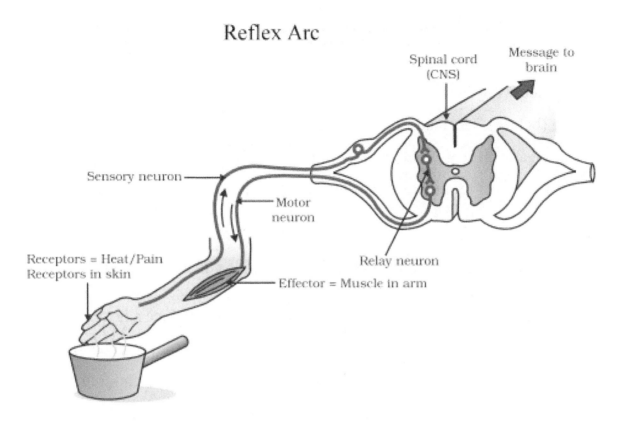

Figure 4.16 Reflex arc

THE PERIPHERAL NERVOUS SYSTEM

This is made up of nerves that branch off from the spinal cord to other parts of the body. The peripheral nervous system allows the brain and the spinal cord to receive and send information to the other areas of the body, which allows us to react to stimuli from the environment.

THE REPRODUCTIVE SYSTEM

The reproductive system is a group of organs that work together to produce offspring (babies). The male and female reproductive systems are made of different organs that carry out different functions. However, these two systems must work together to produce offspring. The reproductive system consists of both internal and external organs for males and females.

THE FEMALE REPRODUCTIVE SYSTEM

The primary role of the female reproductive system is to produce a healthy offspring. It is immature in young females and does not mature until puberty. The average age for puberty in females is 10 to 11 years old but some children can experience pubertal changes from as early as 8 years old. Before puberty, a female is not able to produce an offspring. Some changes that occur during puberty include:

- Breast development
- Pubic hair growth
- Ovaries begin to release eggs (ovum)
- Menstruation
- Armpit hair growth

Female fertility ends at menopause which occurs between 48 and 50 years old on average.

The female reproductive system is divided into internal and external organs.

INTERNAL ORGANS:

Ovaries

This organ produces and releases one ovum (egg) every month. Females have two ovaries, on either side of the uterus. The ovaries also produce female sex hormones such as estrogen and progesterone.

Fallopian Tubes

These are two tiny tubes that connect the ovaries to the uterus. They transport the ovum (egg) from the ovaries to the uterus.

Uterus (womb)

This organ is responsible for the development of the foetus during pregnancy. This is a very remarkable organ that expands during pregnancy to accommodate the growing foetus. After pregnancy it returns to its original size. It is also responsible for expelling the baby from the body during childbirth.

Cervix

This is the lowest part of the uterus. It has a narrow opening that allows sperm to enter the uterus to fertilize the egg.

Vagina

This is a muscular organ where sperm is deposited during intercourse.

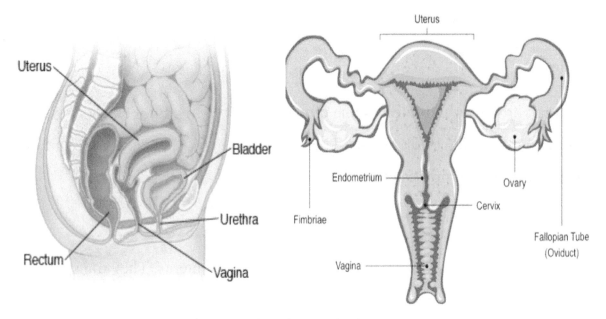

Figure 4.17 Female reproductive system

EXTERNAL ORGANS:

Vulva

This is the outer most part of the female reproductive system. It includes: the vaginal opening, clitoris and labia.

MALE REPRODUCTIVE SYSTEM

The male reproductive system plays a very important role in human reproduction. The male reproductive system matures at puberty which occurs between the ages of 11 to 12 years old on average. Male pubertal changes include:

- Increased facial and body hair
- Enlargement of the penis
- Enlargement of the testicles
- Enlarged larynx (voice box or Adam's apple)
- Production of sperm

Unlike females, males are fertile throughout their lives. They can continue to produce sperm even in their eighties. The male reproductive system is divided into internal and external organs.

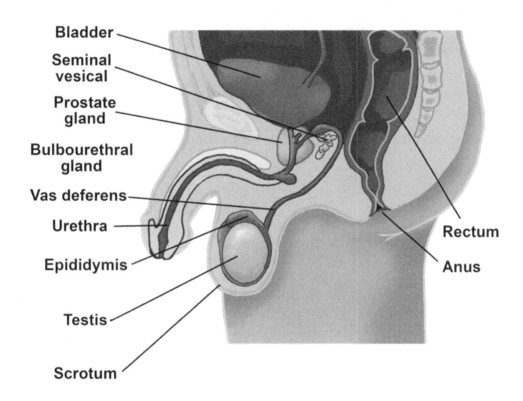

Figure 4.18 Male reproductive system

INTERNAL ORGANS

Testicles or Testes

This is an organ that is responsible for the production of sperm and testosterone, which is the male sex hormone.

Epididymis

The epididymis stores sperm.

Vas deferens or Sperm duct

This is a long tube that transports sperm from the epididymis to the tip of the penis during intercourse.

EXTERNAL ORGAN:

Penis

The penis is responsible for delivering sperm to the female sex organ. Each ejaculation consists of approximately 20 million sperms that compete to fertilize the single egg.

Scrotum

This is a soft pouch that holds the testicles. It helps to maintain the optimal temperature for sperm production.

THE EXCRETORY SYSTEM

The function of the excretory system is to remove wastes from the human body. This process is called excretion. The human excretory system includes: the kidneys, ureters, bladder, urethra and several sweat glands. However, the kidneys are the main excretory organs.

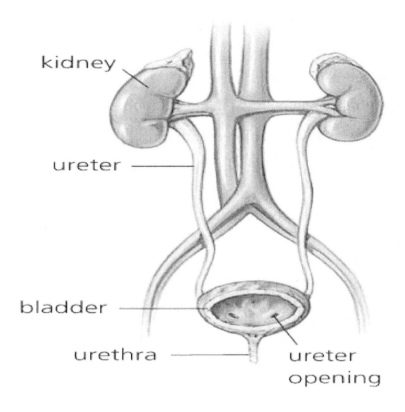

Figure 4.19 Excretory system

The kidneys

Every human being has two kidneys, shaped like a bean. They are the primary excretory organs in the human body and they are located on each side of the abdomen. The function of the kidney is to filter the blood, removing wastes and maintains a balanced internal system. Large blood vessels take blood to the kidneys. The blood is filtered and the wastes and excess water are transformed into urine.

The Ureters

This is a thin muscular tube that carries urine from the kidney to the urinary bladder. There are two ureters, one attached to each kidney. The upper half of the ureter is in the abdomen and the lower half is in the pelvic area.

Urinary Bladder

This is a muscular sac that stores the urine that is made in the kidneys. It is located above and behind your pelvic bone. When it is empty, the bladder is about the size and shape of a pear. The bladder is lined with muscle tissues that allow it to stretch to hold urine. It can hold between 400 – 600ml of urine.

When urine fills the bladder, the muscular wall contracts pushing the urine out though the urethra.

The Urethra

Urine is carried from the bladder through the urethra to the outside of the body.

OTHER EXCRETORY ORGANS

The skin

The skin is the largest organ of the human body. Its primary function is to protect the other organs and tissues of the body. However, it also helps to excrete waste through sweat. In the sweat the body excretes salt and urea.

The lungs

The lungs help in excretion by removing carbon dioxide from the body during breathing and respiration. It also removes water vapour as well.

The Liver

The liver helps in the excretion process by removing the excess fat and cholesterol that are not needed from the body.

END OF CHAPTER TEST

PART 1

1. Describe in detail the movement of food through the digestive system.

_____

_____

_____

_____

_____

_____

_____

_____

_____

_____

_____

_____

_____

_____

_____

2. Explain the functions of the liver and pancreas in the digestion process.

_____

_____

_____

_____
_____
_____
_____
_____
_____

3. Draw and label a diagram of the digestive system.

4. Explain the flow of blood through the human body.

_____
_____
_____

_____

_____

_____

_____

_____

5. Explain the differences between arteries, veins and capillaries.

_____

_____

_____

_____

_____

_____

_____

_____

6. Draw and label a diagram of the human circulatory system.

7. Explain gaseous exchange in humans.

_____

_____

_____

_____

_____

_____

_____

_____

_____

_____

8. Explain what happens to air as it passes through the body.

_____

_____

_____

_____

_____

_____

_____

9. Draw and label a diagram of the skeletal system.

10. Explain how the muscles and bones work together to produce movement.

_____

_____

_____

_____
_____
_____
_____
_____
_____

PART 2

1. Draw and label a diagram of the nervous system.

2. Describe the functions of the human brain.

_____

_____

_____

_____

_____

_____

_____

_____

3. You stepped on a needle and you quickly lift your foot. With the aid of a
   diagram, explain the reflex action.

_____

_____

_____

_____

_____

_____

_____

4. Compare the pubertal changes in males and females.

_____

_____

_____

_____

_____

_____

_____

5. Draw and label a diagram of the female reproductive system.

6. Outline the function of the uterus.

_____

_____

_____

_____

_____

_____

_____

_____

7. Draw and label a diagram of the male reproductive system.

8. Explain how the body excretes waste through the kidneys.

_____

_____

_____

_____

_____

_____

_____

9. Draw and label a diagram of the excretory system.

10. Identify two other excretory organs and explain their function.

_____

_____

_____

_____

_____

_____

_____

_____

_____

_____

_____

CHAPTER 5: MIXTURES

A mixture is a material that is made up of two or more substances that are not chemically bonded together. The properties of the substances that make up a mixture always remain the same. However, the mixture may have new properties. For example, if you pour sand into a glass of water, you have created a mixture of sand and water. Both the sand and the water remains the same and can be separated from each other.

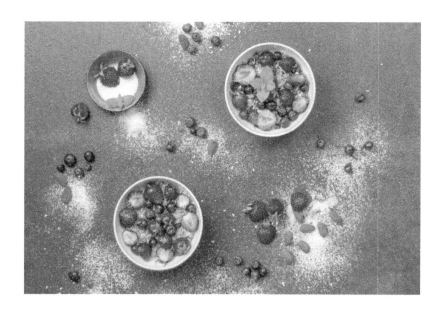

Image 5.1 A mixture of cereal and fruits

Mixtures are classified based on how uniform they are. They can also be classified based on the size of the particles of each component.

Substances that combined to form mixtures include:

- Flour and sugar
- Sugar and water
- Marbles and salt

- Cereal and milk

- Oil and water

- Coffee and cream

- Honey and tea

- Dirt and water (mud)

- Sand, water and gravel (cement)

- Water and salt (sea water)

Other mixtures include the combination of metals to form a new type of metal called alloy. This is done to produce a metal with new properties.

- Zinc and copper becomes brass

- Gold and silver becomes white gold

- Iron and carbon becomes steel

- Copper and tin becomes bronze

TYPES OF MIXTURES

There are two categories of mixtures:

Heterogeneous

This is a mixture in which the components are not evenly distributed throughout the mixture. There are some regions that may have different composition and concentration than other regions. For example: cereal and milk, pizza, blood, gravel, ice in soda, vegetable soup, etc.

Homogeneous

This is a mixture in which the components are evenly distributed throughout the mixture. Examples include: air, sugar and water, rainwater, steel, vinegar and dishwashing detergent.

Mixtures can also be classified based on the size of their particles. They are divided into three categories; solution, suspension and colloid.

Solution

This is a mixture that contains particles that are very small in size. A solution is physically stable and its components cannot be separated by pouring the liquid or substance from one container to another. Examples include: sugar and water, salt and water and rubbing alcohol.

Colloid

This is a mixture of larger particles that are evenly distributed throughout the mixture. In this type of mixture, the substances do not settle at the bottom of the container. Examples of colloids include: milk, salad dressing, mayonnaise and gels.

Suspension

This is a heterogeneous mixture where particles settle at the bottom of the mixture. For this type of mixture the particles are big enough to settle. The components of a suspension can be separated by pouring one substance from the mixture. Examples include: dirt and water, flour and water, and oil paint.

Science Experiment: Mixtures

In this experiment we will investigate different types of mixtures.

Procedure:

1. *Place a sample of salt, sand, dirt and sugar in separate containers.*
2. *Add half cup of water to each sample and mix for 2 minutes.*
3. *Observe and record your findings.*

	Salt	Sand	Dirt	Sugar
Observation				
Type of mixture				
Technique to separate the mixture				

Table 5.1 Results of the mixture experiment

Results

Discuss your findings.

_____

_____

_____

_____

_____

_____

_____

_____

_____

_____

SEPARATION OF MIXTURES

Some common techniques used to separate mixtures are:

Simple Distillation

This is a process that is used to separate two liquids of different boiling points. For example, water can be separated from sea water (salt and water) using simple distillation, because salt and water have different boiling points. This process can be used to convert sea water into drinking water.

1. The mixture is heated to the boiling point of water, which is 100 degrees celsius. This causes the water to vaporize (evaporate).
2. The water vapour passes through a cooled tube that causes it to condense into water droplets.
3. The droplets are collected and the salt remains in the container.

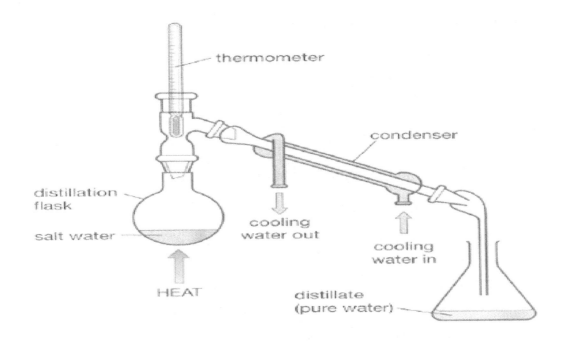

Figure 5.1 Diagram of simple distillation

Evaporation

This is a technique used to separate homogeneous mixtures where there is one or more dissolved solids in a liquid. This process is used in the production of sugar. The mixture is heated until all the water has evaporated and the sugar crystals begin to form.

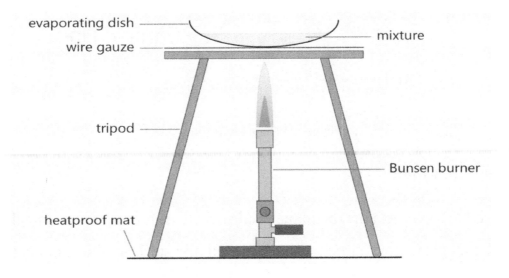

Figure 5.2 Diagram of evaporation

Filtration

This is the process by which solid particles are removed from a mixture of a solid and a liquid using a filter medium. This allows the liquid to pass through but holds back the solid particles. Essentially, it is a method used to separate an insoluble solid from a liquid. For example, water treatment plants use filters to remove sediments from water. This prevents large sediments such a leaves and branches from blocking the pipelines.

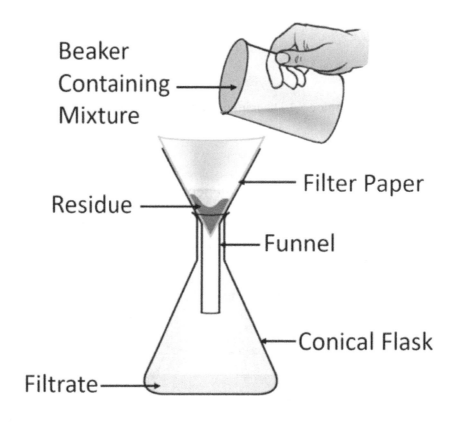

Figure 5.3 Diagram of filtration

Magnetic Separation

This is used to separate a magnetic material such as iron from a non- metal such as sulfur. The magnet attracts iron particles leaving the sulfur in the container.

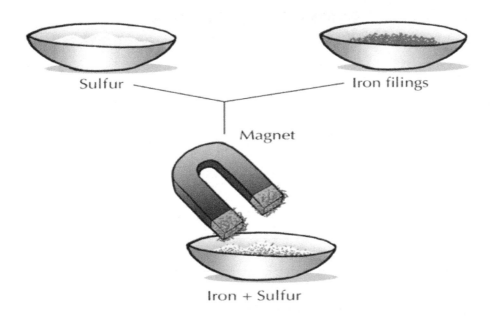

Figure 5.4 Diagram of magnetic separation

Separating funnel

This is an instrument that can be used to separate two liquids that does not mix together. If you try to create a mixture of oil and water, the water will sink to the bottom and the oil will float. This is called an emulsion. The separating funnel allows you to pour off the water, leaving the oil in the funnel.

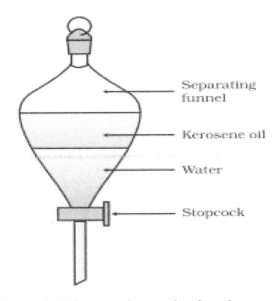

Figure 5.5 Diagram of separating funnel

END OF TOPIC TEST

1. Explain what is meant by a mixture.

_____

_____

_____

_____

_____

2. List three (3) examples of mixtures.

_____

_____

_____

_____

_____

3. Explain the differences between homogenous and heterogeneous mixtures.

_____

_____

_____

_____

4. Categorize mixtures based on particle size.

_____

_____

_____

5. List three (3) examples of colloids.

6. Define the term alloy.

7. List common examples of alloys.

8. You live in Qatar where there is a shortage of fresh water. Describe a separation technique that can be used to convert sea water into drinking water.

_____

_____

_____

_____

_____

_____

_____

_____

9. Your mother is making carrot juice. She blends the carrot with water to make a mixture. Identify the type of mixture and explain a separation technique that can be used to produce a juice that is free of sediments.

_____

_____

_____

_____

_____

_____

_____

CHAPTER 6: DIET

BALANCED DIET

It is important to maintain a balanced diet because your body's organs and tissues need nutrients to carry out their functions properly. You need the right nutrients in the right quantities to maintain a healthy body. Scientists have found that having a balanced diet helps to prevent diseases. Without proper nutrition, you are more prone to disease, infection, fatigue and poor performance. Children with a poor diet are at risk of having developmental problems.

A balanced diet is one that has some of all the basic food groups: carbohydrates, fats, proteins, minerals and vitamins in the right proportion. Nutrients can be classified as macronutrients and micronutrients. Macronutrients include: fat, carbohydrates and protein. Micronutrients include: vitamins and minerals.

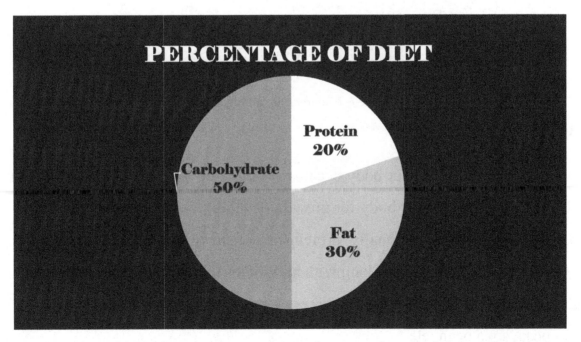

Figure 6.1 Pie chart showing percentage of macronutrients in a balanced diet

MACRONUTRIENTS

Carbohydrate

This is the primary source of energy for your body, providing 55% to 60% of the calories you need. In addition to providing fuel or energy to keep your body active, carbohydrate supports your growth. When you consume too much carbohydrate your body converts the excess into fat which is stored in the body. This can result in obesity. Sources of carbohydrate include: bread, rice, yams, pasta, etc.

Image 6.1 Sources of carbohydrates

Protein

Protein is important for your body because it makes up your skin, muscles, organs and hair. It is used by your body for growth, development, maintaining and repairing body cells. Additionally, proteins make enzymes and hormones that regulate your body functions along with antibodies that help the immune system to fight diseases and infections. The sources of protein include: chicken, fish, egg, pork, peas, soya bean, etc.

Image 6.2 Sources of protein

Fats and Oil

About 35% of the calories you consume should come from fat. Fat supports cell growth, protects your organs and helps to keep the body warm. Additionally, it helps your body to absorb nutrients and produce hormones. Sources of fat include: butter, cheese, oil, meat, etc.

Image 6.3 sources of fat

MICRONUTRIENTS

Vitamins

These are complex substances that are essential for the proper functioning of the body. Vitamins help to convert food into energy and help your body to use protein, carbohydrate and fat. Vitamins are also important in maintaining the health of the immune system, brain and nervous system. There are several types of vitamins, each with a specific role in the body. The vitamins are divided into water soluble and fat soluble vitamins.

WATER SOLUBLE VITAMINS	
VITAMINS	SOURCES
Vitamin B1	Pork, whole-grain or enriched breads and cereals, legumes, nuts and seeds
Vitamin B2	Milk and milk products; leafy green vegetables; whole-grain, enriched breads and cereals
Vitamin B3	Meat, poultry, fish, whole-grain or enriched breads and cereals
Vitamin B6	Meat, fish, poultry, vegetables and fruits
Vitamin B12	Meat, poultry, fish, seafood, eggs, milk and milk products
Vitamin C	Fruits and vegetables, especially citrus fruits, vegetables in the cabbage family, cantaloupe, strawberries, lettuce, papayas and mangoes

Table 6.1 Water soluble vitamins

FAT SOLUBLE VITAMINS	
VITAMINS	**SOURCES**
Vitamin A	Cheese, cream, eggs, liver, dark green leafy vegetables, cantaloupe, carrots, sweet potatoes and pumpkin
Vitamin D	Egg yolks, liver, fatty fish and fortified milk. When exposed to sunlight, the skin can make vitamin D.
Vitamin E	Soybean, corn, leafy green vegetable, liver, egg yolks, nuts and seeds
Vitamin K	Leafy green vegetables such as kale and spinach; green vegetables such as broccoli and brussels sprouts

Table 6.2 Fat soluble vitamin

Minerals

Minerals are essential elements that are required for the optimal functioning of the body. These include, iron, calcium and sodium. Calcium is one type of mineral that forms the structure of and strengthens bones and teeth. Sodium and potassium are important in maintaining fluid balance and muscle contraction. Iron is needed to make red blood cells that transport oxygen. Sources of minerals include: vegetables, milk and liver.

Fibre

Fiber can be found in plants such as fruits, vegetables and grains. It helps to maintain a healthy digestive system. Sources of fibre include: oats, brown rice, whole wheat flour, green leafy vegetables, apples and mangoes.

UNBALANCED DIET

Image 6.4 Cheeseburger

This is a diet that has an excess or deficiency of essential nutrients. An unbalanced diet is caused by poor eating habits or a lack of nutritious foods. The body needs the right amount of nutrients to function properly. An excess or deficiency of a nutrient can result in severe health consequences.

In the short term, poor nutrition can contribute to stress, tiredness and reduce our capacity to work, and over time, it can contribute to the risk of developing severe illnesses such as:

- Obesity

- Tooth decay

- Hypertension (high blood pressure)

- High cholesterol

- Heart disease and stroke

- Type-2 diabetes

- Osteoporosis

- Some cancers

- Depression

OBESITY

Obesity is a medical condition that occurs when a person has excess body fat that might affect their health. Obese persons have an increased risk of developing health problems, such as heart disease, diabetes and high blood pressure. Obesity is measured by your body mass index (BMI). Body mass index (BMI) is a tool that doctors use to assess if a person is at an appropriate weight for their height. The measurement combines height and weight. See BMI chart below.

CLASSIFICATION	BMI
Underweight	<18.5
Normal	18.5 to 24.9
Over weight	25 to 29.9
Obese	>30

Table 6.3 BMI chart

Obesity is diagnosed when your body mass index (BMI) is 30 or higher. To calculate your body mass index, divide your weight in kilograms by your height in meters squared.

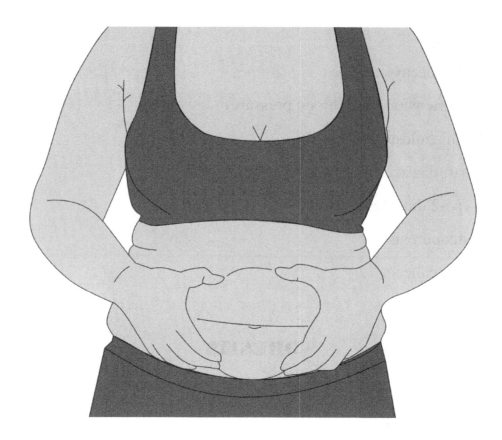

Figure 6.2 Obese woman

There are many reasons why some people have difficulty avoiding obesity. Usually, obesity results from a combination of inherited factors, combined with lifestyle choices. Although there are genetic, behavioral, metabolic and hormonal influences on body weight, obesity occurs when you take in more calories than you burn through exercise and normal daily activities. Your body stores these excess calories as fat.

Contributing factors

The genes you inherit from your parents may affect the amount of body fat you store and where that fat is distributed. Genetics may also play a role in how efficiently your body converts food into energy, how your body regulates your appetite and how your body burns calories during exercise. Obesity tends to run in families. That is not just because of the genes they share. Family members also tend to share similar eating and activity habits.

Causes

Genetics   Overeating   Hormone

Medications   Smoking

Insufficient sleep   Sweetened drinks   Sedentary lifestyle

Figure 6.3 Risk factors for obesity

A diet that is high in calories, lacking in fruits and vegetables, full of fast food, and laden with high-calorie beverages and oversized portions contributes to weight gain. People can drink many calories without feeling full, especially calories from alcohol. Other high-calorie beverages, such as sugared soft drinks, can contribute to significant weight gain.

If you have a sedentary lifestyle, you can easily take in more calories every day than you burn through exercise and routine daily activities. The number of hours you spend in front of a screen is highly associated with weight gain.

Prevention

It is recommended that you get 150 to 300 minutes of moderate-intensity activity per week to prevent weight gain. Moderately intense physical activities include fast walking, cycling, running, skipping and swimming. Focus on low-calorie, nutrient-dense foods, such as fruits, vegetables and whole grains. Avoid saturated fat and limit sweets and alcohol. Eat three regular meals a day with limited snacking.

People who weigh themselves at least once per week are more successful in keeping off excess weight. Monitoring your weight can tell you whether your efforts are working and can help you detect small weight gains before they become big problems.

DIABETES

Diabetes mellitus, commonly known as diabetes, is a metabolic disease that causes high blood sugar. It is a condition that impairs the body's ability to process blood glucose (blood sugar). The hormone insulin moves sugar from the blood into your cells to be stored or used for energy. With diabetes, your body either does not make enough insulin or cannot effectively use the insulin it makes. Untreated high blood sugar from diabetes can damage your nerves, eyes, kidneys, heart and brain. There are three different types of diabetes:

Type 1 diabetes

This is an autoimmune disease in which the body is unable to produce insulin. The immune system attacks and destroys cells in the pancreas, where insulin is made. It is unclear what causes this attack. The body fails to produce insulin. People with type I diabetes are insulin-dependent, which means they must take artificial insulin daily to stay alive. About 10 percent of people with diabetes have this type.

Type 2 diabetes

This occurs when your body becomes resistant to insulin and sugar builds up in your blood. Type 2 diabetes affects the way the body uses insulin. While the body still makes insulin, unlike in type I, the cells in the body do not respond to it as effectively as they once did. This is the most common type of diabetes.

Gestational diabetes

This type occurs in women during pregnancy when the body can become less sensitive to insulin. Gestational diabetes does not occur in all women and usually resolves after giving birth.

Causes of Diabetes

Doctors do not know exactly what causes type 1 diabetes. For some reason, the immune system mistakenly attacks and destroys insulin-producing cells in the pancreas.

Type 2 diabetes, also known as insulin resistance, has clearer causes. Insulin allows the glucose from a person's food to access the cells in their body to supply energy. Insulin resistance is usually a result of the following cycle:

- A person has genes or an environment that makes it more likely that they are unable to make enough insulin to cover how much glucose they eat.
- The body tries to make extra insulin to process the excess blood glucose.
- The pancreas cannot keep up with the increased demands, and the excess blood sugar starts to circulate in the blood, causing damages.

Over time, insulin becomes less effective at introducing glucose to cells, and blood sugar levels continue to rise.

In the case of type 2 diabetes, insulin resistance takes place gradually. This is why doctors often recommend making lifestyle changes in an attempt to slow or reverse this cycle. Type 2 diabetes stems from a combination of genetics and lifestyle factors. Being overweight or obese increases your risk of developing type 2 diabetes.

Risk Factors for Type 2 Diabetes

The risk factors for type 2 diabetes include:

- Obesity
- Family history of diabetes
- Sedentary lifestyle
- History of gestational diabetes.

Effects of Diabetes

High blood sugar damages organs and tissues throughout your body. The higher your blood sugar is and the longer you live with it, the greater your risk for complications.

Complications associated with diabetes include:

- Heart disease, heart attack, and stroke
- Nerve damage
- Kidney damage
- Vision loss
- Foot damage such as infections and sores that are difficult to heal
- Skin conditions such as bacterial and fungal infections
- Depression
- Dementia.

Diabetes can lead to serious medical complications, but you can manage the condition with medications and lifestyle changes.

Prevention and Treatment

Doctors treat diabetes with a few different medications. Some of these drugs are taken by mouth, while others are available as injections.

Insulin is the main treatment for type 1 diabetes. It replaces the hormone your body is not able to produce.

Diet and exercise can help some people manage type 2 diabetes. If lifestyle changes are not enough to lower your blood sugar, you will need to take medications. Healthy eating is a central part of managing diabetes. In some cases, changing your diet may be enough to control the disease.

Here are a few things you can do to delay or prevent type 2 diabetes:

- Get at least 150 minutes per week of aerobic exercise, such as walking or cycling.

- Reduce saturated fat and refined carbohydrates in your diet.
- Eat more fruits, vegetables, and whole grains.
- Eat smaller portions.
- Try to maintain a normal body mass index (BMI)

UNDERNUTRITION

Undernutrition refers to when a person's diet does not provide enough nutrients or the right balance of nutrients for optimal health. Malnutrition refers to both undernutrition and overnutrition. Undernutrition can lead to serious health issues, including stunted growth, developmental delay, marasmus and kwashiorkor. The causes of undernutrition include: inappropriate dietary choices, a low income, difficulty obtaining food, and various physical and mental health conditions. If a person does not get the right balance of nutrients, they can also have malnutrition. It is possible to have obesity with malnutrition.

Every country in the world is affected by one or more forms of undernutrition. Combating undernutrition in all its forms is one of the greatest global health challenges. Women, infants, children and adolescents are at particular risk of malnutrition. Optimizing nutrition early in life, including the 1000 days from conception to a child's second birthday, ensures the best possible start in life, with long-term benefits.

People of lower economic status are more likely to be affected by different forms of malnutrition. Also, undernutrition increases health care costs, reduces productivity and slows economic growth, which can perpetuate a cycle of poverty and ill health.

The effects of undernutrition include:

- Muscle wasting
- Physical disability
- Developmental delays
- Increased risk of infections
- Fatigue
- Difficulty concentrating

Marasmus

This is a severe form of undernutrition resulting from a deficiency in protein and energy rich nutrient such as carbohydrates. Marasmus is characterized by muscle wasting and loss of body fat.

Kwashiorkor

This is another serious form of undernutrition resulting from a deficiency in protein but adequate energy. Protein wasting in kwashiorkor results in fluid accumulation and abdominal distension.

Rickets

This is a bone disease that results from a lack of vitamin D, calcium or phosphate. It causes the bones to be very thin and easy to fracture.

Scurvy

This disease results from a deficiency in vitamin C. It is characterize by skin sores and gum disease.

Prevention

To prevent undernutrition, the diet must consist of a wide range of nutrients from a variety of food types. Older adults, young children and people with chronic illnesses may need additional care to ensure that they obtain the nutrients they need. Research suggests that some of the most effective ways to prevent malnutrition include: providing iron, zinc and iodine pills, food supplements and nutrition education to populations at risk of undernutrition. You can also help to prevent malnutrition by maintaining a diet with a variety of foods that include: enough carbohydrates, proteins, fats, vitamins, minerals and water.

END OF TOPIC TEST

1. Explain the differences between a balanced and unbalanced diet.

_____

_____

_____

_____

2. Give an example of a balanced and an unbalanced diet.

_____

_____

_____

_____

3. List the functions and sources of protein.

_____

_____

_____

_____

_____

4. List the functions and sources of carbohydrates.

_____

_____

_____

_____

_____

5. Identify three (3) fat soluble vitamins and three (3) water soluble vitamins and list three (3) sources of each.

_____

_____

_____

_____

_____

_____

_____

_____

6. List the causes and effects of obesity.

_____

_____

_____

_____

_____

_____

_____

_____

7. Your cousin has a BMI of 35. He wants to know how to stay healthy. How do you advise him?

_____

_____

_____

_____

_____

_____

_____

_____

8. List the causes and effects of type 2 diabetes.

_____

_____

_____

_____

_____

_____

_____

_____

_____

9. List the causes of undernutrition.

_____

_____

_____

_____

_____

10. Explain the differences between marasmus and kwashiorkor.

_____

_____

_____

_____

_____

CHAPTER 6: DRUGS

A drug is any substance which, when taken into the body, changes the body's function either physically and/or psychologically.

LEGAL DRUGS

These are drugs which are not prohibited by law. They include drugs for medical use as well as intoxicants such as alcohol. They are sold over the counter in various retail stores or food-suppliers. Examples of legal drugs include: stimulants such as caffeine found in soft drinks, coffee and tea, and nicotine found in all tobacco products. Alcohol is another common drug that is legal to consume. It is widely available in several different forms such as run and beer. Medical drugs include: pain killers, diabetes medicine and cold medicine.

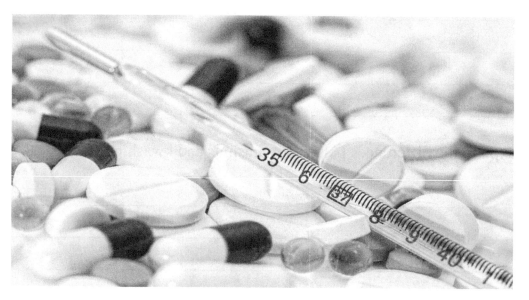

Image 7.1 Drugs

ILLEGAL DRUGS

These are drugs that are forbidden by law. Different illegal drugs have different effects on people and these effects are influenced by many factors. This makes them unpredictable and dangerous, especially for young people.

Types of illegal drugs:

- Cannabis (marijuana)
- Cocaine
- Ecstasy
- Heroin

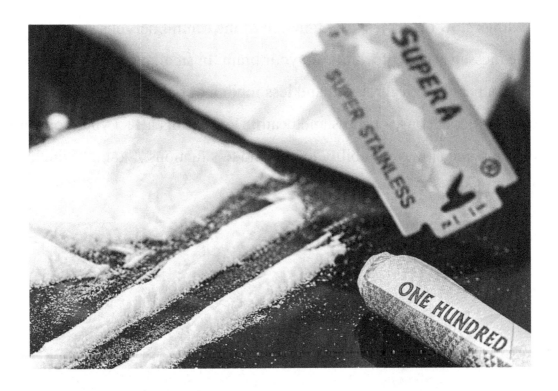

Image 7.2 Cocaine

EFFECTS OF DRUGS ON THE BODY

Drugs can have short-term and long-term effects. These effects can be physical and psychological and can include dependency, which leads to addiction.

You may act differently, feel differently and think differently if you have taken drugs. You may also struggle to control your actions and thoughts.

Drugs affect your body's central nervous system. They affect how you think, feel and behave. There are three main groups of illegal drugs: depressants, hallucinogens and stimulants.

Depressants

These drugs slow or 'depress' the function of the central nervous system. They slow the messages going to and from your brain. In small quantities depressants can cause a person to feel relaxed and less inhibited. In large amounts they may cause vomiting, unconsciousness and death. Depressants affect your concentration, coordination and slow your ability to respond to situations. Examples include: alcohol and heroin.

Image 7.3 Alcohol

Hallucinogens

These drugs distort your sense of reality. You may see or hear things that are not really there, or see things in a distorted way. Other effects can include emotional and psychological euphoria, jaw clenching, panic, paranoia, upset stomach and nausea. Examples include: marijuana and magic mushroom.

Image 7.4 Marijuana plant

Stimulants

Stimulants speed up or 'stimulate' the central nervous system. They speed up messaging to and from the brain, making you feel more alert and confident. This can cause increased heart rate, blood pressure, body temperature, reduced appetite, agitation and sleeplessness. In large amounts stimulants may cause anxiety, panic, seizures, stomach cramps and paranoia. Examples include; caffeine, nicotine, amphetamines, cocaine and ecstasy.

Image 7.5 Cigarette contains nicotine

PRESCRIPTION DRUGS

We take drugs (medications) to diagnose, treat, or prevent illnesses. They come in lots of different forms and we take them in many different ways. You may take a drug yourself, or a healthcare provider may give it to you.

Drugs can be dangerous, even when they are meant to improve our health. Taking them correctly and understanding the right way to administer them can reduce the risks.

It is important to take only the dosage described in the prescription label or other instructions. Dosage is carefully determined by your doctor and can be affected by your age, weight, kidney, liver health, and other health conditions.

Adverse events, or unwanted and negative effects, can happen with any drug. These effects can include an allergic reaction or an interaction with another drug you are taking.

If the medicine is a prescribed drug, the prescribing physician will give you personalized instructions on its use. The instructions for use are attached to the package in a pharmacy. In over-the-counter medicines sold in pharmacies, the instructions for use are in the package.

DRUG ABUSE

Drug addiction is the chronic uncontrollable drug seeking behavior despite negative effects on the body and social life. Examples of addictive drugs include: nicotine, alcohol, cocaine and morphine. People abuse drugs for several reasons including:

- To feel good - Some drugs can produce and intense feeling of pleasure.
- To feel better - People abuse drugs when they are sad to help them feel better.
- To perform better - People take drugs to improve their performance especially in sports.

Risk Factors for Drug Abuse

Image 7.6 Say no to drugs

Some individuals are more likely to become drug addicts than others. The risk factors for addition include:

- Aggressive behavior in childhood
- Lack of parental supervision
- Poor social skills
- Drug experimentation
- Availability of drugs at school
- Community poverty

Protective Factors against Drug Abuse

People with the following characteristics are less likely to become addicted to drugs:

- Good self-control
- Parental monitoring and support
- Positive relationships
- Good grades
- School anti-drug policies
- Neighborhood resources

Effects of drug abuse

- Addition
- Difficulty sleeping
- Increased risk of accidents
- Cancers
- Heart disease
- Mental illness
- Death

END OF TOPIC TEST

1. Define the term drugs.

_____

_____

_____

_____

_____

2. Explain the difference between legal and illegal drugs.

_____

_____

_____

_____

_____

3. List three (3) examples of legal and illegal drugs.

_____

_____

_____

_____

4. Explain the effects of illegal drugs on the body.

_____

_____

_____

5. Compare the effects of stimulants and hallucinogens.

6. Identify three (3) risk factors for addiction.

7. List three (3) ways to prevent addition.

Congratulation! You have successfully completed the grade 6 science curriculum.

Made in the USA
Las Vegas, NV
25 January 2024

84775349R00083